SURVIVING THE EREMOCENE

ISBN: 978-1-962405-32-4
Library of Congress Control Number: 2025941007

Sheila-Na-Gig Editions
Russell, KY
Hayley Mitchell Haugen, Editor
www.sheilanagigblog.com

SURVIVING THE EREMOCENE

poems

Chuck Salmons

Sheila-Na-Gig Editions

Advance Praise

Chuck Salmons writes of ordinary life—marriage, family, work—but finds ways to release tension, anger, and joy so that we come out in a new place that is both emotionally and aesthetically satisfying. His brilliance, for all his technical skill, is to give us a sense that we are all in this together, that he's out there for all of us, figuring out how to make sense of muddled, disappointing, and sometimes glorious lives. We may not become better human beings after reading *Surviving the Eremocene*, but if not, the fault will be our own. Salmons offers us our chances, poem by compassionate, wise, and ironic poem.

—George Bilgere, author of *Central Air*

Chuck Salmons is a fine, fine poet with his feet firmly planted in the Midwest—even when his eyes are raised to the sky, even when he is physically far away. He brings together a love of science, and a love of the unknown; he mixes global headlines with neighborhood playgrounds, all with humility and tenderness for our complicated, conflicted country. In a series of deeply moving family poems, he examines the weight of limited possibilities, the compromised choices of working-class life. His rich imagery gives depth to the hard-earned emotions of these poems. They are memorable and heartfelt—readers will feel their own hearts responding in this age of loneliness, reminding us that ultimately, we are not alone, that we need each other to survive.

—Jim Daniels, author of *An Arrogance of Trees*

Acknowledgments

Chiron Review: "Life Is but a Dream House"

Common Threads: "My Son Practices the Ollie 540," "Utility"

Encore 2020: "My Father Cursed"

Evening Street Review: "Gambit," "How to be Grateful," "I Give You This Ring," "Louie," "Merlot," "Surviving the Eremocene"

I Thought I Heard a Cardinal Sing: Ohio's Appalachian Voices: "Ode to Scioto Trail Swim Club," "On the South End, Too"

Illinois State Poetry Society (Member Poems online): "Sanibel Stoop"

The Main Street Rag: "Poem for Bob Ross"

Northern Appalachia Review: "At the Dawn of the Anthropocene"

Poets to Come: A Poetry Anthology: "Gathering Leaves With My Son"

Pudding Magazine: "Kinds of Blue," "Perspectives," "Rock," "Saving Breath," "Snowshoeing," "Striking the Colors"

Sheila-Na-Gig online: "At the Bottom of the Exit Ramp," "How Not to Spell *Cello*," "Poem for the New School Year," "*Why is it so?*"

Slippery Elm: "Choices"

The poet is grateful to the following friends and fellow artists who offered invaluable critiques of many of the poems included in this book: Rikki Santer, Sandy Feen, Kathleen Burgess, Chris Minton, James Borders, Susann Moeller, Via Laurene, Nik Macioci, and the late Anna Soter.

for all those struggling to ensure their own survival

Poems

I.

II.

Eremocene: "Age of Loneliness"; derived from the Greek *eremo* (lonely, bereft) + *kainos* (new)

Popularized by naturalist E.O. Wilson, the term defines an epoch during which humans will experience a great sense of existential and material isolation resulting from the mass extinction of many species of other living things.

I.

Surviving the Eremocene

The world never feels fallen, because we grow
accustomed to the fall.

—Brooke Jarvis

You felt it early in life—

    when a friend sucker punched you,
    your other friend laughing along
                as you sulked from the
    playground—

    the morning *Challenger*'s debris
    traipsed the uncluttered sky
    like burning bits of doubt
    littering your mind about one day riding rockets—

    the afternoon your father forgot
    to pick you up from soccer practice,
    sending you and your brother searching
                for a pay phone.

And later, that same plunging—
    when students fled Columbine,
    when you saw bodies drop

    from smoking monoliths
                the day the towers fell, and too
    when pitch scorched and blackened
                the Gulf sky above BP's *Horizon*.

Then again when you held your mother's hand
as the needle flooded her veins with chemicals
                to crush cancer in her lymph nodes.

Now, that worm in your stomach
rises into your chest again as you watch—

Charlottesville, Minneapolis, Kenosha—

walnut and hickory trees bear meager fruit,
heirloom tomatoes wilt as mere blossoms—

fewer butterflies and honeybees
          bounce in the prairies.

Above you, magenta clouds loom,
concealing stars
          once looked to for guidance.

Locust trees lob their leaves to the wind
like confetti at the end of summer's parade
as you gaze at clouds scudding
through a sky falling farther away
and wonder why the divine did not gift us
                              with wings.

Poem for the New School Year

Russia Strikes Playground in Kyiv After Blaming Ukraine
for Crimea Bridge Attack
          —Headline from Vice.com, October 10, 2022

Overhead, against the blue scalp of October sky,
two olive drab Hueys rumble aloft
loaded with Army reservists on a training flight.
Meanwhile, on the Liberty Elementary playground,
a jungle gym bounces with boys maneuvering
the monkey bars. Too big for the apparatus,
they bend their legs at the knees to avoid dragging
their feet in the mulch bed below. They swing,
stutter bar to bar, wing spans too great
for such small gaps between grips.
Who would tell them they are far too old
for this play? Who would push them so quickly
into manhood, those long years burdened
by more questions than answers. Even now,
when their flesh has begun to sweat and stink,
their desires checked only by body-to-body
collisions on basketball courts or football fields,
they find simple joy in the sway of long legs
above the ground, like soldiers in those choppers
expecting nothing but a soft landing.

My Son Practices the "Ollie 540"

Never mind the pendulum
nature of the half-pipe,
my son gliding
side
to
side
against its walls.
Rather look above its rails
where he spins like a dervish
and tumbles time after time
only to stand smiling.
Undeterred, he soon flies again,
eyes focused, arms askew,
singular of purpose.

He once told me
the name of this new stunt
and I laughed, thinking
only of portly Mr. Hardy
twirling with his thin, clumsy partner
on a dusty street way out west.
But it's no joke,

this daredevil feat.
For this is how I want him to move
through the world—
like a samara whirling
gracefully through the air.
Diligent to learn, eager
to master such moves,
to change
                    direction,
to skate on and tackle
the next big trick.

Louie

At age ten, Louie Donovan outran everyone.
In his South Side Devils uniform, he looked to score
with every touch of the football. *Louie the Laser*,
Coach Slatzer called him. He lined up
under center, at wideout, or in I formation. He burst
through a hole on the 22-Dive in a blue blur,
would-be tacklers never ready for such speed.

At age ten, Louie and our team ground it out
for the Under-10 title at Cooper Stadium—
brass and marble trophies, pizza party after.
At age ten, Louie's talent was rare, beautiful,
like a green streak of sky at dusk. But soon
the Devils disbanded. Like free agents,
players signed with neighborhood teams.
Louie and his family moved to Easthaven. We fell

to a better team the next year. I walked off the field
for good, waving at Louie who sat beside his father
on the wooden bleachers, the two of them sporting
our rival's colors. A ball cap loosely covered his head
swollen by a tumor. His eyes gazed into October
sunset. Some opponents can't be outrun.

Perfection

for Darrin Kortyka

It's a young man's dream, the one
we've grown old enough to concede
is unobtainable, unwarranted

except in the year we were born,
when Shula and the Dolphins won
it all, start to finish, vanquishing

what would become your beloved
Steelers who reaped the glory of their
Immaculate Reception the week before.

It calls into question the will of the divine,
how it reconciles a playful penchant
for tinkering while appearing impartial.

Did your parents watch Super Bowl VII
expecting the same result, as you lay
warm in your mother's belly? Would my own?

It took the NFL 52 years to produce perfection.
On the eve of our own half centuries, we accept
flawlessness as something only nature can spawn—

hyacinth blossoms perfuming April air,
a suncrisp apple's tart sweetness,
its flesh rose and gold in your hand—

ocean surf pounding Cannon Beach,
Haystack and The Needles black against the Pacific
horizon, emerald sea glass awash at your feet—

your son's laughter as he shrugs yet
another of your would-be tackles in
a friendly backyard game of football—

those moments between moments
when we relinquish our incessant need to know,
succumb to an ineffable impulse to let go.

Merlot

Planning to cook for her,
I scour my mother's kitchen,
search the fridge
for food still holding shape—
crowded condiment bottles,
leftover beer, soda, molding cheese.

So we dine out—
a rosemary loaf, basil
penne on blue plates,
a bottle of her favorite merlot.
This night her appetite is strong,
but we know it won't matter
because with chemo
everything tastes metallic.

Lifting her glass with a wink
she says, *The poet who drinks sour wine
will always write a fermented line.*
We laugh, our glasses raised
to praise her doctor, the kind nurses
who hit her vein the first time,
every time. She pretends to savor
the sauce, lauds the wine—*smoky,
full-bodied, a merlot with memory.*

She's right about the wine.
A glass or two loosens her tongue.
Four years since the divorce
and she wants someone to be there
when poisons pump through her veins.
She's looking for a reason
to fill the fridge with fresh food,
someone to cook with,
someone to share the merlot.
A son can only do so much.

At the Bottom of the Exit Ramp

The bearded man summons another
morning of strength to smile and wave,
hefts a ragged cardboard remnant,

spelled out in black marker the plight
of himself and his partner, the woman
sitting hoodie up beneath the pole light.

Rancid as a dirty armpit, stuck as a rusted zipper,
he has no time for candor, no patience
for the pinecone crumble of asphalt alleys

litter strewn with broken bottles, yogurt cups,
the occasional needle—so he has pitched their tent
here near a bustling exit. His mission: expediency,

hastened by the ever-changing traffic signal.
His goal: another day of handouts—
bottled water, a few bucks to buy a sandwich,

another blanket to keep them warm
beneath January's lazy eye moon.
I offer an apple and orange to nourish them

and the life stirring inside her,
to usher them closer to spring, its hyacinths
carpeting the exit in gold and green

and above their tent, a river birch
weeping, branches bursting with catkins,
about to cast its seed to the wind.

Choices

*On January 22, 1973, the Roe v. Wade decision
was handed down by the U.S. Supreme Court.*

It was a Monday, a good day
to be conceived. And a good chance I was.
At least fifty-fifty, my mother claims,
her wry grin hovers above a glass of cabernet.
In South Columbus, that day was warmer
than expected. I imagine my parents

leaving Marion-Franklin High School, together
in my father's primer gray '62 Ford Fairlane,
windows down. My mother is sixteen, a sophomore,
and laments an Early American History exam
she didn't study for. My father's bitching
about his early morning civics class,
one of the few remaining in his senior year,
its tome textbook lying in the backseat.
He tunes the car radio to 1230 WCOL-AM
where Johnny Rivers belts out some
"Rockin' Pneumonia." Maybe they find that
empty lot behind Columbus Motor Speedway,
toss *Principles of Democracy* to the floorboard,
and practice the backseat boogie.

My mother couldn't explain the vomiting,
and her bout with palsy did not ring any bells.
She says the term *abortion* was foreign,
unheard of in this matriarchal family.
My grandmother—an ordained minister
in the Church of God—knew the symptoms
and upon the doctor's confirmation, dictated
that her daughter be married, before her
belly gave away another family secret.
With that utterance, my mother had no choice
in the matter. *I have no regrets,*
she tells me. *None at all.*

Bruckner Road

At Chessie System rail yard, diesels tugged
reefers and coal cars, chugged in syncopation—
creeping, rusted shadows
        loaded   emptied
            loaded   emptied
and the street of my childhood reached a dead end.
On summer nights, thick air carried clacks and
pings through my bedroom window
as rail workers toiled, tough-handed and gritty,
eyes strained as lumbering locks snapped,
steel wheels gleamed in lamplight.

I dreamed of hopping a box car
bound for redwoods and Big Sur,
charging surf of Maine, or warm Gulf waters—
anywhere but one-block-long Bruckner Road.
On Saturdays, mean stock cars rumbled
roughshod at Columbus Motor Speedway
where friends and neighbors, backyard drivers,
sped past twilight into incandescent
glow of low-rent racetrack spotlights,
V-8s growling, drowning
the soft trill of crickets beyond shutters.

Our fathers shined on those nights—
mechanics and NASCAR wannabes
trading day-job pickup trucks for home-built stock cars.
They worked OT, scraped together
enough green to keep engines purring,
wheels turning. They scrimped
enough to fill the tank for family cars
and road trips, racing late into the night,
eyes red behind the wheel, fixed
on the fast lane, the coal-black highway
stretched before them like another unending,
unanswered prayer.

My Father Cursed

when he toiled and tinkered
with family cars and trucks.
His head, arms, torso swallowed
below the front fender, legs
splayed as he cussed the '82 Mustang
with its metric nuts and bolts
and parts assembled in Canada.
His curses commingled with clanging
wrenches and sockets hitting the garage floor.
Breaking the stubborn silence
of a spark plug that wouldn't budge,
he let fly profane phrases
bluer than his '77 Silverado.
He cursed the drudgery of auto repairs,
greasy fingernails and grimy forearms,
stained denim, blackened rags.
But he relished rewards of money saved.
He boasted of besting his mechanic,
Uncle Ephraim, who lived next door
and swore with aplomb.
Together they cursed their careers,
the slog and grind of shovel to dirt,
hammer to nail. They batted bad language
across the chain link fence like a shuttlecock,
foul flourishes blazing summer Saturday nights.
And we their sons surrendered
to the seduction of their diction,
marveled and memorized masters' words,
eager to take the court or field
during Monday morning recess
and bellow what we'd learned,
the real lessons lost on us
until years later when we must
mend our own bruised knuckles,
bend to the will of our bones.

Close Encounter

When my wife turns to me
and asks if I've ever seen a UFO,
I tell her about a night
Dad and I came home
after fishing the Big Walnut
(as always, empty handed),

and I saw five orbs glowing,
floating toward the tree line
in a musical dance like the five notes
scientists play to welcome the visitors
before sending Richard Dreyfuss
on a journey that will demonstrate
Einstein's greatest theories.

A formation like so many have seen,
as they are quick to explain
during middle-of-the-night TV shows
about Nessie or Yeti or Bigfoot,
or how the pyramids were really built
by ETs that copulated with our ancestors
and bred a new human ingenuity.

The object passed beyond the trees,
over our neighborhood
as if to land at Grandmother's church,
a chaste, white building
where on Sundays parishioners
           sang, prayed, and
fell to the floor, writhing, wriggling,
and speaking an ancient language,
possessed by the tongue of the divine.

Or perhaps by the guttural utterings
of intergalactic visitors—

Klaatu barada nikto—
a language of the heavens
brought to us from some distant planet,
passed down through generations
except the meaning was lost in translation,
and sometimes the visitors return
to quell our arrogance and remind us
why we're here.

I was never compelled
to sculpt a model of Devil's Tower
or drive into the desert alone,
bewitched behind the wheel.
But when my wife looks at me,
as Terri Garr looks at her husband
from across the dinner table,
disbelieving yet loving him still,
I tell her that when we caught fish
we always released them.
I tell her, on that night
I nearly hopped my bike and
rode through the streets chasing aliens.
Instead, Dad walked into the yard with me,

and we watched the strange lights
dip below the trees. His truck
and my bike sat mutely in the garage,
and we simply let it go.

Why is it so?

for Julius Sumner Miller

When physics is your business,
business can't ever be down.
Nor can a child's curiosity, especially
at age eleven when his body begins
to bloom. So, he hides away on summer
afternoons in his grandparents' bedroom
to watch and learn from you on the 19"
black-and-white Zenith tuned to PBS.

He imagines himself standing with other
boys in the television studio with you,
while his grandmother sits in the living room,
folding laundry and watching *The Young
and the Restless* on a color console.
Her puritan heart cannot justify her appetites,
will not lend her the words to explain her
throbbing desire for Victor Newman
nor the ache her grandson feels at any time,
all the time.

              Instead, she prepares his lunch—
fried boloney sandwich, small bag of Fritos,
an icy can of Faygo red pop.
He sits mesmerized by the week's installment
of *Demonstrations in Physics*, enthralled
as much by your enthusiasm and diction
as by your experiments, reminding viewers—

> *The experiments I will do are*
> *absolutely trivial in their nature,*
> *but absolutely profound in their meaning.*

He does not yet know he will spend a lifetime
pondering such claims. Still, it is your own

enchantment that compels him to tune in,
that fuels his own longing for learning
and a welcome distraction from those other
thoughts about Trinity, the neighbor's granddaughter,
how she ducks away with him beneath the ancient
honeysuckle bush and shares the fruity smack
taste of her lips. He wants to ask you, Professor,
about those desires roiling inside him.
You are a man and surely felt the same urge,
the same unseen force, a kind of magnetism.

> *When you deal with Nature, you must*
> *make such requirements as she demands,*
> *or she will not do what you want done.*

But neither you nor the ones he loves can tell
him where to find the courage to do so.
For now, he settles to sate the other
passion you awakened in him,
the one that will drive him for years
asking that same question behind all others.

Poem for Bob Ross

You have the power to move mountains.
—Bob Ross

The story goes you painted each scene
three times. It's 1988 and off camera,
your first attempt sits like a trail blaze
guiding you, leading us into Alaskan backwoods.
A little phthalo blue, some Van Dyke brown,
a touch of crimson, and behold—
the Yukon rises from your canvas.
Who played more: you or the paint,
titanium white breaking into snowcaps?
By the end of the show, this offspring
will leave us longing to see the final painting
you will create after cameras stop rolling.

The story also goes you hated your hairdo,
the trademark curly, cost-cutter perm
that might have been envied by my grandmother
and every other housewife from Hamlin, West Virginia.
Betty scrimped all her life, even after moving
to Columbus, getting remarried, starting over.
She saved every glass bottle she could find
walking to the bus stop, where she waited
for the COTA No. 4 to take her north
to Main Street to meet my grandfather
after his shift in the machine shop.
At Kroger, Bill & Betty claimed bottle deposits,
saved the cash to pay for travel
back to the mountains that birthed her—
mountains much older, more weathered
than those that arose from your imagination.
She grew up eager to leave poverty
and her son-of-a-bitch first husband behind
after my father was born. She might tell you
how beautiful the Appalachians are to look at,

to drive through, how they calm and reassure
when your destination seems so far away.
She would explain they rarely give second chances,
let alone third, and harden a man so much
he will do his damnedest to keep his woman
down, trapped in those hollows where streams
and trees could paint her into obscurity.

How Not to Spell *Cello*

In our family the only instruments that mattered
were guitars and drums, maybe a banjo
plucked with perfection by Dr. Ralph Stanley
on my grandfather's AM radio every Sunday
after service at Hilock Baptist Church.
Finer stringed instruments were expensive
things that other kids learned to play—
kids whose parents worked for banks and
accounting firms. Who could afford
dance lessons and ski club memberships
or listened to Händel, Bach, and Brahms.
Kids raised Catholic or maybe Episcopalian,
their sermons steeped in the beauty of
Latin chants and not hellfire, damnation.
They walked out of stone cathedrals
with stained-glass windows feeling purified.
We walked out of our chaste, white church afraid
even to ask real questions, the ones our
school teachers wanted to answer but
refrained for fear of retribution by parents
who saw education as a sanitized means to
an end where their children grab a diploma
and head either to recruitment office or steel mill.
My parents played Elvis, the Stones, Skynyrd.
No piccolos or violas in their tunes.
No cellos either, with or without an *h*.
When I stepped off the stage during fifth grade
spelling bee at Stockbridge Elementary,
I knew Adam Fisher would be the last student
standing. He would receive his trophy and
a handshake from the school principal,
and walk off the stage, into the arms
of his parents well dressed and quietly smiling
as if they had been moved by yet another
performance by the Columbus Symphony Orchestra.

Saving Breath

In my family my job was not
to be like my father,
although I tried

to enjoy fishing from the banks
beneath bright July sun,
all day without a bite;

to relish the recoil
as his .30-30 kicked
in my unsteady hands;

to savor a cigarette,
smoke stench tarnishing
my clothes and kisses.

But I couldn't help but smile
when we worked together
landscaping his clients' lawns—

carving a clean edge
as the spade's cold blade
ripped sod and soil,

stacking rough stone
into wending, winding walls,
hefting a trowel,

staking a young maple,
spreading warm, moist mulch
and breathing its vinegary scent,

then sweeping sidewalks.
I admired each fresh, new look
as I wiped my calloused hands

clean. We would drive home,
recline with the setting sun,
few words between us

all day, saving our breath
for those moments—most of our lives—
when the real hard work needed doing.

Summer 1984

In the photo, my brother leans against my father's
shoulder, platinum hair slivered beneath
the orange bill of a plastic mesh trucker cap,
blue eyes still, mouth and brow in a scowl,
eight-year-old arms tanned in a striped tank-top.
My young father's eyes hide behind aviator shades.
His mustache walrus tusks drape
the corners of his stoic mouth, bronze face
not yet creased. I want to tell my brother to smile,
to stick out his tongue, to spin that hat around.
Twenty years from now, he and my father will have
the same stern look of men hardened by work,
callused hands, gnarled skin leathered
under anvil sun. I want to tell them
how lumber and bricks have no scruples.
How after years of cutting, digging, lugging, lifting,
their backs will stiffen, knees pop when they stand.
I want to warn them about countless hours of OT,
family trips ending in divorce, laughter dulling
with questions about love and the divine, their hearts
yearning for someone to show them the way.

Ode to Scioto Trail Swim Club

for Roy Bentley

In South Columbus in the 1980s, American boys and girls
could have their pick of music to groove to, strutting
poolside during Late Night Swim at Scioto Trail Swim Club,
assuming their mothers and fathers could afford the price
of membership with blue-collar paychecks, Reaganomics
funding a war on drugs, and Republicans spewing
western rhetoric, pressing the Soviets to tear down the wall.

But what did middle and high school kids care about taxes
when there were skin and skimpy swimsuits to ogle
from the deep end, water polo street rules in the diving area.
We were mesmerized by how Old Man Blakeman's
daughter—already at sixteen—filled out a one-piece.
Music bounced through chlorinated air.
Sometimes we grumbled, sometimes we dug it.
Depends on the neighborhood we hailed from.
Our elders called for Cash, Kenny, or Loretta,
they too steeped in hill-country roots and rigor.
My brother and I argued Duran Duran versus Dokken.
Friends from L.A.—"Little Africa" our parents called it—
would thump Big Daddy Kane or Eric B. and Rakim.
Soon we got Run D.M.C. splashed with a little Steven Tyler
and Aerosmith, the formula for racial harmony set
before us on MTV.

        Except the right people weren't watching,
weren't listening, unwilling to consider their misconceptions.
But we were daring, took our digs and disagreements downhill
to the undersized basketball court with rigid rims that kicked
out long rebounds, frequent fast breaks, or to the ping-pong
table where a well-honed backspin meant you were the one
calling *Next!* long into evening. Cannonballs from the high dive
were never out of style, concession hot dogs never out of stock.

Only summer could burn out when Labor Day weekend signaled a new school year. At the back of the bus, Walkmans pumped "Brass Monkey," the hip-hop funk of inner-city Jewish boys bursting beyond Brooklyn's boundaries through our ears, into budding spaces where anything was possible.

Under the Covers

Early in the year I was born,
Tricky Dick declared
peace with honor in Vietnam
and the end of the draft.
My father could keep his wavy,
shoulder-length hair,
Fu Manchu, suped-up Chevelle.
He was off the hook, free to explore
the world on his own terms

except for the child
in his young bride's belly
about to blossom like a full moon
above the horizon of their lives.
That would be my mother talking.

My father might have said
the moon thrusts itself upon him
like an incessant neighbor
who can't take a hint.
He would rather cloak its light
in a suffocating shroud of clouds,

the way years later he sometimes pinned
me in play beneath a blanket,
let me struggle, squirm, so I might learn
what it means to yearn
for a chance to breathe easy, to drift
unnoticed like a wisp of cloud
on a moonless night.
He didn't say that.

But he could have.

In Praise of the French Burnt Peanut

You the demon seed—
pimply, umber skin,
hard as gravel
and just as forgettable
except when Mom took us shopping.
At JC Penney Outlet store
we stood in line, cart full
of Rustler denim jeans,
bright polo shirts, over-the-calf socks,
and there you were, tempting us,
hanging in the check-out rack
among the Bazooka bubble gum,
Brach's caramels, and circus peanuts.
Mom granted us a bag each

and riding home we tore
into the gleaming cellophane
and sucked sweet candy shells,
bumpy pebbles rolling
on our tongues like defective marbles.
We dared to bite down,
the crunch rippling through
our molars before you succumbed
with soft, salty peanut centers.

Were you really French?
Were you really burnt?
Were your peanuts really Spanish?
Such questions mattered
about as little as shopping
for new fall wardrobes,
mattered so much less than learning
that the rarest of oddities taste
sweeter than any routine.

Grandfather Teaches Me to Make Biscuits

Potatoes and green beans simmer,
four hours now. Pork loin sizzles.
First comes flour and soft butter
      in a glass bowl etched
by his mother's modest diamond.
He stirs slowly. A wooden spoon
turns the mixture into itself like a wave.
Then he pours milk from memory,
his eye measuring the fleshy mound.
He dusts a sheet of foil with flour
and kneads a lumpy sphere.

He tells me his mother learned to cook
after her mother died. At age eight,
she stood on an overturned dynamite box
brought from the mines by her brothers.
The boys returned each night,
faces and arms black with Ohio coal dust,
and devoured biscuits and beans.

He tells me that in Korea
beans were always bland,
biscuits were always cold and hard
like the winters in Chosin.

He says *always bake biscuits in an iron skillet,*
      like the one his mother handed down.
He says *always cook beans slowly—*
      with potatoes and pork,
      with the care a farmer takes to grow them.

His hands shiver and press dense dough
into a pale pancake. With an empty tin can
he cuts biscuits, slides them into the oven.
Our arms and brows bead with sweat.
The ceiling fan stirs a salty scent.
Grandfather talks. Biscuits begin to rise.

Striking the Colors

Swashbucklers make dubious heroes.
At least, that's what no one tells
a kid from the south side of Columbus.
When Dad shared home movies,
he gave friends and family a sneak peek
at intermission, like a coming attraction—
Against All Flags starring Errol Flynn
flying across the screen on 8-mm film,
a promo reel Dad snagged from a movie house.
I was hooked.

Flynn infiltrated the enemy armada
and fought the pirates of Madagascar,
against all flags of the privateer fleet—
galleys, galleons, and sloops.
No one swung from a mizzenmast
like him. He swooped in,
his rapier danced and clashed
as the projector ticked and flashed.
I needed more.

At Halloween, Dad and I dressed as pirates,
his Anthony Quinn to my Errol Flynn.
Mom scuffed my face with black make-up,
faux stubble beneath a scarlet bandana.
Donning a cardboard cutlass
wrapped in aluminum foil,
I buckled my swash street by street to loot
my own sweet swag.
Together we sailed house-to-house,
plundered treasure wrapped in silver and gold.
I brought it home, buried it
in my belly. Then one summer, a parley.

Verbal volleys between my parents
stopped. Dad raised the white flag,
loaded his pickup with the movies
and a suitcase full of worker blues.
Mom got the house, the boys, costumes
stowed away like rigging in her cedar chest.

On the South End, Too

for Hanif Abdurraqib, after his poem
"All the White Boys on the Eastside Loved Larry Bird"

We loved him on the South End, too,
where our parents and grandparents identified
with hick-ness, they, too, born and raised
in the whites-only hills of Kentucky, West Virginia,
deep hollows where there were no fields
for football, baseball—just a utility pole
tall enough to nail a piece of plywood,
mount a hoop above a patch of gravel and dirt
alongside trailers our relatives reside in still.

We loved him because he loved the game.
We loved him because when Isaiah offered
the olive branch, he accepted it.

In my neighborhood, our elders would have broken
that branch across their knees, burned it,
used it as a switch across our backsides
for even thinking about inviting guys like you
into their homes. But we knew better,
knew the color of a man's skin meant nothing.
Only his game mattered.

It was the game that bonded us.
It was the game that taught us how to be men,
to say what you mean, mean what you say,

and be ready to back it up
when you lace up the high-tops, step
onto the asphalt, the concrete, shirts versus skins,
and take your opponent one-on-one
hard to the hoop on a July afternoon,
he and the sun double-teaming you,
their breath hot on your bare shoulders.

II.

Snowshoeing

Before he could afford good boots, my father rose on raw winter mornings, packed a modest man's lunch—black coffee, ham sandwich, tomato soup—and warmed camel-colored, faux-leather Texas Steer boots in our oven. Then he laced them over two pairs of thick, red-toed cotton socks (couldn't stand wool—*too itchy, too sweaty*) and greeted frozen Ohio mud with the same ambivalence he carried for his job. But his trick worked, kept his feet toasty and dry in the muck and slush, kept the blood flowing, if only for a few hours. Many years north, under a bald, blue sky, I trek vacant hills near Big Bay, thankful for wool socks, insulated boots. Sweat seeps from my pores, soaks my skull cap. I wonder, had he better boots, would my father have embraced the cold as I do, welcomed its blue tinged world, stinging the lungs, each breath rising into still, frigid air only to vanish, like imprints swept away by wind and snow.

Spotting the International Space Station Flyover

On a night so cold
stars eat the Earth,
it appears without fanfare.
Our neighbors sit snug
in their warm homes
watching reruns while we stand,
audience of two, in snow
boots on the edge
      of a frozen wetland
and applaud with gloved hands
as the ISS rises southwest,
brighter, more stable than
the frigid suns beyond its reach.

It tracks with quiet grace,
like a soloist prolonging
a chord from her cello,
solitary note drawn from the gamut.
In the symphony of sky
others take second chair—
Orion, Jupiter, the Seven Sisters,
      even the moon yields
center stage for but a movement.

The chamber of new instruments
passes overhead, its players
recording the music of our universe,
then fades like a favorite song.
We trek home, your arm in mine,
eager for the playback.

Rock

Stone masons make bad guitarists,
      their muscle-bound hands lumber,
pick stiff notes that fall hard on ears,
      like limestone stacked piece by piece
to keep out the cool crowd
      to which my father never belonged—
dreamers who need more than rhythm,
      who dance with streamers,
scalps dressed in scarlet feathers,
      stage light flickering off sequined shoes,
who seek only rapture, not sculpture.

When I was young, my father plucked his six-string
      on Friday nights, The Standells' "Dirty Water"
a warm-up before unleashing his fingers
      to improvise songs without names
and seemingly without end. He played
      long into evening. Mosquitoes and moths danced
against the front screen door, lured more
      by melody than table lamp glow.

Now his music lies buried
      by the hardened history of a landscaper's toil.
Had he followed his heart's song
      and joined the Navy, his hands might be slender still,
fingers flitting from string to string
      freeing notes deep within.
He might smile and sway, strumming
      a seasoned song of a thousand nights at sea.

Branches

Autumn dusk rises,
pale green afterthought
of a passing storm.
In an orchard on the edge
of town,
　　　　my son and I pick apples.
We meander row upon row,
inhale sweet, pomaceous
aromas that hang among trees
plump with suncrisp,
goldrush, winesap.

As a boy I climbed
trees Grandfather planted,
maneuvered braided branches
splayed out, resplendent,
like spindles of a nebula.
I fetched fruit
golden and dappled,
each skin a sky
　　　　painted with stars.
Universe in hand,
I bit and tasted
sweet secrets at its core.

Now Grandfather's trees are gone,
my own limbs too long
for narrow navigation
but strong enough
to lift my son
　　　　so he may climb.
And behind a broken shroud
of nimbus clouds,
the gibbous moon glows,
shadows his slow ascent
　　　　branch by branch.

How to be Grateful

You are content to soak sunlight
flooding the Gate 3 seating area,
ignore the smattering of children's voices
rising above cool conversations,
one-sided and predictable on this side of
the digital divide. On Thanksgiving eve,
airport televisions sit black—
talking heads banished to the back of
our contemplations—foreshadowing
Friday's mass hysteria to hold
the latest gadget or gaudy bauble.
You sip slowly the coffee in hand,
take a book of poems from your carry-on
and commit yourself to Wright's words,
imagine yourself swaying in the same hammock,
cowbells clanging against the Minnesota horizon.
Then, behind you, gleeful whistling—
a tune familiar but uncertain,
and it occurs to you that such a sound is rare,
as rare as Wright's final line. Truly—

who whistles anymore?
You struggle to recall when you last pursed
your lips and let ring a melody to match
sunshine warm against your cheek.
You remember your grandparents swaying
on the porch swing next to you,
your grandfather whistling long
into evening after Saturday supper,
the old silver maple enticing you
to climb, to find yourself high enough
to see rooftops of mid-century homes
lining the block, neighborhood dogs roaming
their territories in August heat, backyard
gardens lush with tomatoes, peppers, cucumbers,

apple and cherry trees laden with ripening fruit.
Tomorrow, many families will flounder
in false promises of plenty and kindness.

For now, passengers begin to board
the plane that will carry you south,
into the welcoming home of an old friend,
where you will play a game of chess,
share stories about his immigrating from China,
how you helped him to learn English,
how he helped you be a better chess player.
You will struggle to regain a bit of optimism
about the future awaiting his daughters.
And who knows, you might even whistle.

I Give You This Ring

harvested from the heart of a mountain,
taken with pride for its rare beauty
and commingled with lesser metals—
nickel or silver—cast into a narrow band
fit for a poor man's salary.
Its crown of crushed jewels sparkle
less pure than the gold, but their brilliance
swayed Grandfather's beloved enough
to say yes to a lifetime of simple jewelry,
a single income, South Columbus home
with a vegetable garden, fruit trees,
a vine whose Concord grapes
Grandmother turned into jelly to spread
onto homemade biscuits baked in
the tired gas oven of a galley kitchen,
its lone window framed with lace curtains
yellowed with years, grease,
as dingy as the ring scuffed and dulled
because she never took it off,
even to knead the dough.

At the Dawn of the Anthropocene

at Ferncliff Peninsula National Natural Landmark,
Ohiopyle, PA, dedicated 1973

The trail winds beneath hemlock, magnolia,
through an ocean of ferns. Rhododendron
blossoms echo the Youghiogheny whitewater
meandering through the Laurel Highlands.
Yellow blazes march us among plants out of place,
their seeds brought northward by the river
from Maryland and West Virginia like immigrants
into this acclimatized gorge whose thickened warmth
trickles down our spines and soaks our shirts
in July heat hazed by wildfire smoke.

We trek past moss-strewn sandstone
outcrops stamped with scaley traces
of *Lepidodendron* and fossil roots,
giant trees lost to deep Earth time.
We pass trunks of American Beech, bark
once smooth now etched by humans who
give little thought to health and less to history.
Ahead, a young couple stops along the trail,
the woman, her face unwrinkled,
keeps lookout as her partner carves their initials,
his hand guided by hubris. We pass them,
say nothing, offer a simple look in the eye
more of disappointment than disdain.

Farther along we see an area fenced off,
its sign explains how restoration is at work,
how the deer gorged themselves,
rendered the zone fruitless. We speak
softly about the Dust Bowl and deforestation,
mountain-top mines, nuclear testing.
How a few hundred miles north in Ontario,
our everlasting mark on the planet is revealed

in lake sediments tainted with atomic evidence.
We wonder, where are the fences for the beeches?
Who will tame us? Millenia from now,
who will unearth and collect our fallen remains
locked in bedrock, our identities imprinted
like so many limbs of an extinct species.

After a Lecture on International Efforts to Discover the Higgs Boson

All evening I wandered
     during the physics professor's PowerPoint,
imagined the "God Particle" rippling
     through dark space of the auditorium,
entangling my ganglia,
     rendering me numb.
But mostly, I looked forward to my kitchen,
     to black tea and a blood orange.
Now, its spongy heft yields
     as I score the dimpled skin,
wedge my thumb between pith and peel,
     reveal and relish its supple flesh.
I ponder the Big Bang as bright
     citrus splashes my nostrils.
Sticky juice coats my fingers.
     Pulp explodes with every bite,
swells in my mouth before dissolving
     into nothingness.
Laws of physics demand its sugars fuel me,
     its acid guard my cells against foreign bodies.
Somewhere in deep recesses of the infinite,
     the Higgs boson balances our universe,
breaking symmetry, spurring fruit to grow
     from trees. We savor their succulence
and ponder what's left
     after the last sweet slice is swallowed.

The Old Neighborhood

after "Strawberry Fields Forever"
by John Lennon & Paul McCartney

Rose-tinged clouds loom above my arrival
early morning, hours before a memorial
service for an old friend, where our stories
synthesize, flow in low-fi, out of tune
like Mellotronic music fluttering,
a wobble in the sound of our laughter.
From the car radio Lennon laments,
                              Living is easy with eyes closed

but driving these familiar streets even easier,
the presence of absence marks every corner.
Stockbridge Elementary, where I flourished,
is gone, playground & asphalt courts plowed under.
No more basketballs glow orange
against blue July skies or bounce in & out
of the headlamps sidelining our fastbreaks.
                              It's getting hard to be someone

In its place the City has planted an urban forest,
oaks & maples burnish this October sunrise
like gifted students gathered in an open-air classroom,
rising taller than those rusty hoops we cherished,
tempting, encouraging us to climb.
                              No one I think is in my tree

Vanished too my grandparents' house,
gardens & grapevines, even the trees uprooted,
paved over, gut-rot scent of decay washed clean
by time and what some in America call progress.
                              But you know, I know when it's a dream

Now an old girlfriend has passed. We too, past.
But it's okay,
                              Nothing to get hung about

because forever is a neighborhood
in mind, a street like Bruckner Road
where we still run arm in arm,
through shadows between streetlamps,

Nothing is real

where I still run my fingers
through strawberry blonde locks,

Forever

where we steal behind her father's tool shed,
let our burgeoning lips caress.

Let me take you down

Skylab

Skylab roared into orbit wounded and doomed,
damaged at launch, its mission plagued
by problems, fulfilling few promises
with its eyes aimed sunward. My parents, too,
turned away from their dreams—
my mother's belly swelling as she walked in white
down the aisle toward my father who stood near
the altar sporting a robin-egg-blue tuxedo, ruffled shirt.
They did not know their journey would end
like the slow degradation of a satellite's orbit—
cramped quarters testing their camaraderie
like Cold War rivals struggling to cooperate,
avoid mutual destruction. In low Earth orbit,
one learns to love simple conveniences,
to cherish a view of home without creased
edges, moments when loneliness nudges
you to look past your partner's peccadillos,
find a common cause to keep the peace
for watchful eyes, the gravity of every move,
every word witnessed live on closed-circuit.

Kinds of Blue

after Miles Davis

I.

My father comes home, alone
to a house with no history
to call his own.
A second divorce complete,
he sets to painting walls,
carpeting floors, stripping
smoke-stained wallpaper,
replacing locks.
He drinks a Heineken and phones
my mother for advice
about draperies, lighting,
how sunlight filters through
the blue-in-green leaves
outside, into his living room
at sunset, and blinds him
from what lies just beyond
the windowpane.

II.

To be closer to my brother,
his children, my mother has moved
again—another house behind her
in a history of heavy lifting,
every downsizing a garage sale,
truckful of trinkets, memorabilia
mingled with vintage bric-a-brac.
She will adorn the walls with photos
to make it feel less empty
and field calls from my father,
the only man who holds meaning
beyond the blood burning within,

who still gifts her a poinsettia
every Christmas, which will wither
in the months that follow
like a blues without a refrain.

III.

So what does a man do
when those he loves see all blues?
When the portrait of our lives
is no masterpiece
but merely a sketch.
When all we have are improvisation
and the promise of a few wrong notes
in this, our only rehearsal.

Helga and You

after Farm Road, *by Andrew Wyeth, 1979*

Her face a lingering lobe,
a sliver of cheek.
Her neck glows egg yolk
gold against the dark meadow,
splits her coppery hair into two braids.
The ridge barren before her,
save a shadowy stand of trees
looming like bad memories
against the sparse sky, Helga gazes
not at the road veering off
like an afterthought, but at a fruitless frontier.
She is a Laura Ingalls Wilder heroine
searching for a childhood home.

You devoured those books
as a girl, in the back yard
beneath the pin oak
where his drunken shouts fell
on distracted ears, and traded
one bumpy ride for another,
riding with the Ingalls
across the prairie states
in a covered wagon. You endured
brown-bottle winters,
watching the road before you
wind uphill, eyes fixed,
like Helga wondering
what's beyond the trees.

Recovery

My friend Paul does not write poetry
but spends his days in recovery
banging out a new addiction
article, pouring himself into a podcast.

He could take pride in his strides
to overcome his frailties—and he should—
but humility gets the better of him.
He shares his propensity for pop culture

and obsession with James Bond
movies with his two sons.
They listen to the opening themes
on vinyl, vote for their favorites.

From Shirley Bassey's wry "Goldfinger"
to McCartney's anthemic "Live and Let Die,"
they sing together, croon each tune
and rip their air guitars to shreds.

They relish in the fandom
passed from fathers to sons,
wondering, but never aloud,
what took so long.

Life is but a Dream House

at Fallingwater, Mill Run, PA

Stairs and terraces cascade down the hillside,
    eurhythmic echo of Bear Run spilling
        into Youghiogheny rapids.

I thought it would be bigger, this weekend getaway
    for a wealthy Pittsburgh family. Such is its reputation,
        luring visitors from around the world,

including a Belgian couple we make as fast friends—
    he an architect, she a photographer,
        drawn to this uniquely American mecca.

Their easy smiles and French accents bubble
    through thick summer air. We share
        their delight for Wright's clever details—

window corners without mullions, sandstone
    outcrops jutting into a living room, a canopy
        cantilevering a walkway, a swimming pool

fed by a mountain spring. The docent reminds us
    how constant water flows from the hills,
        the house prone to decay, like nations

and dreams, despite the designer's vision,
    the builder's best intentions, the owner's steadfast care.
        We move deliberately from space to space,

compressed and released, like rhododendron
    blossoms that burst open in woods around us.
        The blurred line between inside and

outside unfolds in subtle ochre and Cherokee red.
    We tour and talk, take in "The View"—
        you know the one—the house

hanging in apparent harmony with its host site.
    We snap a photo, stand in awe, content with the idea
        simply to live in the guest house, relish

light music cast by sun through single-pane windows,
    creek song tumbling through our ears.
        Ushered by a security guard, we are last to leave.

We hug one another, exchange email addresses,
    part in friendship. We exit in opposite directions.
        No one will ever build a house like this again.

Beneath the Brecksville-Northfield Bridge, Cuyahoga River

You in your yellow slicker, paused
near the retaining wall, gaze at
the Cuyahoga flowing through its narrows—
too swift to reek of fish rot and muck,
too loud to heed a chill stirring among the trees.

How could you not recall Roman aqueducts,
their great arches spanning
Italy's valleys and gorges, carrying water
to the eternal city from ever greater distances?
What city would you call home?

It might be the same for that stranger
standing on the opposite bank
close enough for you to see wrinkles
at the corners of his eyes, which stare
back, searching for recognition,
a casual wave or welcoming smile.

Would you leap in to save him
or watch him be carried away
like a Visigoth invader—cries hushed
by whitewater, fate handed over
to this conduit for the world,
its towering indifference.

Houston to Santa Fe at 36,000 Feet

We sit trapped in this lightning rod
with wings, tempting the flashes that paint
high clouds hung like smoke from tribal fires
burning to call forth ancient gods.

We anticipate a hard touchdown in a land
with names that chant you breathless—
Kasha-Katuwe, Cochiti Pueblo,
Apache plume, Indian paintbrush,
prickly pear, ponderosa pine.

Somewhere in the desert, a song waits
for us to learn, to sing with coyotes
long into evening, to carry back
and share with our tribes when the sun sits cold
and the earth gleams with torpor.

We've come to expect little from prayer,
from rituals that ache with days
of tearing ourselves away from
a course we're not used to taking, wandering
through darkness like the great river below
toward a destination we only think we know.

Eclipsing the Distance

Eclipse Day 2024
Plano, TX

In the corona of memory,
loves we've lost glow
like prominences, cool loops
tethered to the burning,
internal dynamo of our longing.
Here among friends, I watch
the slow eclipse of our only Sun
high above the Lone Star State.
You do the same so many miles north,
the totality of our experience
mere minutes apart, our joy
a shared anticipation, immersed
in a moment repeated with new witnesses
afar. I would reach across the space
between us, take your hand,
gaze upon the mercurial ring
and ponder the nature of light,
how it bends, evades gravity
with grace, how we perceive it
carrying us through
all our days and nights together.

Desert Song

for Steve Abbott

Outside Albuquerque, the desert sprawls
like tattered sheet music
written for ancient instruments
few play anymore, and so
you are left with its stillness—
harrowing soundtrack for the wretched
splendor of landscape, urging you
to open yourself to its solemn song,
to its questions, which are your questions,
which you've been trying to answer for years
because you learned long ago which
questions are worth asking while she sat with you,
squat on the concrete curb, burning leaves
together, breathing smoke faint as
a smudge of cloud on the New Mexico horizon,
both of you longing for answers,
for what eludes you still
hidden among the broken mesas,
in the heart of the great river,
those vast desert sunsets behind you.

Poem for Your Father's Passing

Consider a drive through the countryside,
its hills, moraines, and eskers gather
moment by moment, hug the earth,
until you're free of the mirror of time.
Only with your eyes open can trees shed
their dead leaves and horses gallop,
unbridled, tamed by a long, white fencerow.
Strangers who wave, whose faces blur
in the rearview looking back at you—
they are the never again that awaits
you at the end of this unfamiliar road.

One Year On

My grandfather's home is a kingdom
in ruins—dilapidated siding,
lawn reclaimed by stray seed and samara.
The key still unlocks the door.
Claws scuffle in the attic. Musty
stench of mold and mildew, a problem
unsolved to his very end.
On the carpet, a dark stain
marks the space that claimed him—
I still see him lying face down,
arms at his side, dead before
he hit the floor and broke his nose,
another pain he never felt.

The bank wants this house
no more than we do.
Soon the city will have its say,
raze the roof and all that bears its weight,
cut down the aged apple trees,
grade and seed the plot,
leave the lot bare again.
A new family may find it suitable,
build their own home,
plant new trees, till a garden.

I may drive by some day,
stop and say hello, shake hands
with the owners, share stories
of backyard barbecues, maple trees shading
the deep lot, rows of tomatoes,
half-runners in the garden,
porch swing swaying in the half light of dusk.
Children will laugh again, climb trees,
suck sweet peaches, tart cherries,
sugary juice coating their sticky fingers.

Uncorked

Somewhere during the slow sunset
exit from Napa Valley, where wine woos us
from bottle to vine, we decide to stop
for one last tour and tasting.

Alpha Omega Winery stirs—wedding party,
stretch limo, gleaming Beemers and Benzes
lining the lot. We lean into a hi-top table,
peruse the menu, its lingo a litany

to lure us with its libations. We order,
toast decades of friendship, prepare our mouths
for notes of oak, vanilla, tobacco—
leather, truffle, anise—a mineral finish

to echo the terroir—deep, dark
cherry on the nose—a hint of hibiscus—
long legs trailing the supple curve of the glass—
tannins puckering our tastebuds—

a wine with old world charm—
surely the best cabernet we'll ever taste.
We chuckle, curious about the sommelier
assessing so many sensory experiences

at once. We're eager for the lingering
tingle in our fingers, grateful for our wives
who have carted us—as so many times before—
all day through this valley of oenophiles.

We ponder the lofty language, the lengthy list,
like life, full of sweet promise and twisted
shortcomings, flavors to remember
and flavors to forget, for better or worse—
all of it bottled up and beautiful.

Gathering Leaves with My Son

He tells me the whoosh and crackle is
a pile of crumpled paper,
a million crinkled report cards
with rotten grades, ready to bag and burn
before parents read them
and impose punishment.

I tell him the crash is ocean surf
washing ashore its flotsam, lifeless
leaves with edges mimicking sea shells—
scalloped oak, serrated maple and birch,
and gingko fanning out lobes
like two halves of a clam.

I explain even detritus finds a purpose—
squirrels sculpt their dreys and dens
with dead leaves, fallen twigs,
hollowed husks of acorns and walnuts
rot, feed the soil, sea shells harden
into limestone for bridges and buildings.

But how to tell him what will become
of our own ash and bones…
How to prepare him to scatter what's left
of me—partly among lichen and moss,
partly at sea.

We keep raking up metaphors—
fleeting testaments to moments
when we still need one another
to push back against the world,
defy its tendency to cast aside
what it deems no longer useful.

Sanibel Stoop

You find yourself bending
to the first sun-bleached lucine
big enough to stand out
from dainty debris of the sea.

Surf recedes, and low tide reveals
a trove of treasure washed ashore.
You feed the fever
you've been fighting for years,

pluck from the craggy beach
prizes few of us want—
missing spines, flared lips, jagged remains—
vestiges of a violent past,

the tide cutting and pounding,
resounding in the names:
ark, whelk, conch, coquina.
Each stoop returns in your hand

shells weathered, pitted, broken
and in your eye, pride
in such perfect imperfections.

Utility

Her clammy hand in mine,
my mother listens anxiously
as the oncologist says to wait
and watch closely the nodes
swollen again in her neck.
In six months, scans will reveal
the truth of her condition.
Until then, she will wonder
if her body has worn itself thin.

My father, on the eve of retirement,
laments arthritic hands and knees,
arms scarred from decades of labor, injury—
his body an extension of shovel, pick, spade.
His clients must seek a new craftsman
to sculpt their lawns and gardens,
while his own—once lush
with hydrangeas, catmint, chrysanthemum—
become overgrown, borders
creeping, ragged with crabgrass.

Each morning a ripple climbs my spine.
Twist of torso, turn of the head,
I place my feet on the floor
and rise, stretch—each bend,
each lunge, each deep breath loosens
stiff-hinged tools of my own
fleshy, flawed machine,
its utility beholden to what lurks
in blood and bone, until the body speaks,
deems it time to chase another form of joy,
slippery and golden in the crook of an arm.

Gambit

Atop Hogback, you see the U.P. stretch
its wilderness beyond Marquette, Lake Superior
an open sea of shimmering cobalt and cold cruelty.
Where better to best a classmate in a game of chess
this last Saturday before you defend your thesis
and set to proving your father wrong about you leaving
a high-paying job that gave you nothing but ambition
for something else. This May day, sunlight warms
the blossoming north woods, paper birch
forests awaken to an unfolding of possibilities.
And neither you nor your opponent are sure
of your next move. You should not be still
in this game—his skills better than yours,
more calculating, more studied.
His brow dispels a presumed authority.
You breathe the cleanest air you've ever inhaled,

save that ferry ride from Marblehead to Kelleys Island,
crossing Lake Erie with your grandparents
who took you and your brother everywhere
they journeyed, both of you nestled into the capped
bed of Grandfather's white Chevy pickup
truck loaded with camping gear and a cheap
magnetic checkerboard with plastic pieces.
The gulls grew raucous, waters calm
enough for you to wander the upper deck
and stumble upon two strangers playing
an odd game with exotic pieces, astounding moves.
You pause, watch, listen, a new lexicon
wrapped in the drawl of English accents—
En passant. Castle. Checkmate.
A shaking of hands as the defeated departs.
The winner invites you to sit down. You explain
you do not know how to play.
He offers to teach you, possibilities mesmerize.

You envision the kings fat and lazy,
the queens nimble and pretty
as you make your first move. Soon the lake is memory,
hum of ferry engines lost in breeze.

Now vanquished, you are ready to shake hands,
hike down the mountain.
You reflect on the strategy that failed you,
weigh the wrong moves. And the right ones.
You look forward to a stronger king, a wiser queen.
You will ask her to marry you, to carry you awhile.
And she will. And she does. Even now.

Notes

pg. 14: "Surviving the Eremocene"—The epigraph is from Jarvis' article, "The Insect Apocalypse is Here," published in *The New York Times*, November 11, 2018.

pg. 54: "At the Dawn of the Anthropocene"—*Anthropocene* is an unofficial term used by some scientists to identify the geological period of time during which human activity has been the dominant influence and has had significant, and perhaps irreversible, impact on Earth systems, including climate, ecosystems, and landscapes.

pg. 56: "After a Lecture on International Efforts to Discover the Higgs Boson"—In the Standard Model of Particle Physics, the Higgs boson (or "God particle") is the fundamental particle associated with the Higgs field, which gives mass to other fundamental particles such as quarks (which make up protons and neutrons) and electrons.

About the Author

Chuck Salmons has served as a leader for the Ohio Poetry Association for more than a decade. His poems have appeared in numerous journals and anthologies, including *Chiron Review, The Fib Review, Evening Street Review, The Ekphrastic Review, Main Street Rag, Pudding Magazine,* and *I Thought I Heard a Cardinal Sing: Ohio's Appalachian Voices.* He has previously published three poetry collections: *Stargazer Suite* (11thour Press), *Patch Job* (NightBallet Press), and *The Grace of Gazing Inward: Poems in Response to the Art of Alice Carpenter* (Dos Madres Press). Chuck received a 2018 Ohio Arts Council Individual Excellence Award for poetry, and he performs with the poetry trio Concrete Wink. chucksalmons.com

www.ingramcontent.com/pod-product-compliance
Lightning Source LLC
Chambersburg PA
CBHW020803130626
46554CB00006B/2300